I0817058

DINOSAURS

STEGOSAURUS

BY STEPH GIEDD

An Imprint of Abdo Publishing
abdobooks.com

abdobooks.com

Published by Abdo Publishing, a division of ABDO, PO Box 398166, Minneapolis, Minnesota 55439.

Printed in the United States of America, North Mankato, Minnesota.
102023
012024

Cover Photo: Shutterstock Images
Interior Photos: Jose Antonio Penas/Stocktrek Images/Science Source, 4–5; James Kuether/Science Source, 6; Akkharat Jarusilawong/Shutterstock Images, 8; Thierry Monasse/Getty Images News/Getty Images, 9; Mark Garlick/Science Photo Library/Alamy, 10; Roger Harris/Science Source, 12–13; Richard Bizley/Science Source, 14; Universal Images Group North America LLC/De Agostini Picture Library/Alamy, 17; Daniel Eskridge/Shutterstock Images, 18; Universal History Archive/Universal Images Group/Getty Images, 20–21; Red Line Editorial, 23; Ernest Bachrach/John Kobal Foundation/Moviepix/Getty Images, 25; Vladimir Bolokh/Shutterstock Images, 26; Herschel Hoffmeyer/Shutterstock Images, 28–29

Editor: Marley Richmond
Series Designer: Mary Shaw

Library of Congress Control Number: 2023939659

Publisher's Cataloging-in-Publication Data

Names: Giedd, Steph, author.
Title: Stegosaurus / by Steph Giedd
Description: Minneapolis, Minnesota: Abdo Publishing, 2024 | Series: Dinosaurs | Includes online resources and index.
Identifiers: ISBN 9781098292690 (lib. bdg.) | ISBN 9798384910633 (ebook)
Subjects: LCSH: Dinosaurs--Juvenile literature. | Prehistoric animals--Juvenile literature. | Stegosaurus--Juvenile literature.
Classification: DDC 567.90--dc23

CONTENTS

Stegosaurus ate plants such as ferns that were low to the ground.

CHAPTER 1

SLOW AND SPIKY

A small group of *Stegosaurus* (STEHG-uh-SOHR-uhs) munch on some plants and small trees. The dinosaurs have kite-shaped plates running along their backs. The plates start on their necks and end on their tails.

Stegosaurus was slower than many predators, including *Allosaurus*. But *Stegosaurus's* tail helped keep it safe.

Their tails end with four long, sharp spikes. These spikes help protect them from **predators**.

Suddenly the peace is broken. An *Allosaurus* crashes through the trees. It is looking for its next meal. The slow-moving *Stegosaurus* **herd** scatters as quickly as it can.

The predator closes in on a *Stegosaurus*. But the *Stegosaurus* is ready. It whips its tail around. It pierces the *Allosaurus* with its spikes. The hurt *Allosaurus* limps away. The *Stegosaurus* goes back to its meal.

Terrifying Thagomizers

The Far Side was a comic. One cartoon from 1982 showed a group of cavemen in a classroom. They were learning about *Stegosaurus*. The teacher said its tail was called the thagomizer. This was because another caveman named Thag had been killed by a *Stegosaurus* tail. In reality, people were not alive at the same time as dinosaurs. But many scientists today call *Stegosaurus* tail spikes thagomizers because of the comic.

The National Museum of Nature and Science in Tokyo, Japan, has displayed a *Stegosaurus's* tail spikes.

Jurassic Dinos

Dinosaurs roamed Earth millions of years ago. The time when dinosaurs were alive is split into the Triassic, Jurassic, and Cretaceous periods. *Stegosaurus* was alive during the late Jurassic period (201 million to 145 million years ago). The first *Stegosaurus* lived about 155 million years ago.

Modern history and science museums display dinosaur bones. The Royal Belgian Institute of Natural Sciences displays a *Stegosaurus* skeleton.

At one time, all land on Earth was part of a supercontinent called Pangaea. During the Jurassic period, Pangaea broke apart. This caused Earth's environment to change. Scientists believe that the environment changed too much for *Stegosaurus* to survive.

The asteroid that crashed into Earth filled the sky with dust and blocked the sun. It changed the environment too much for dinosaurs to survive.

The dinosaur went **extinct** about 145 million years ago, at the end of the Jurassic period.

The Cretaceous period ended about 66 million years ago. Evidence shows that an asteroid crashed into Earth. Volcanoes erupted too. These natural disasters are believed to have caused the last remaining dinosaurs to go extinct.

Fossils from these periods of Earth's history were left behind. That is how people today know about dinosaurs. Scientists called **paleontologists** study fossils. Paleontologists share what they learn about dinosaurs with the world.

Further Evidence

Look at the website below. Does it give any new evidence to support Chapter One?

Stegosaurus

abdocorelibrary.com/stegosaurus

Stegosaurus's plates were arranged in two rows along its back.

THE ARMORED DINOSAUR

Stegosaurus was a large dinosaur. It was about 9 feet (2.8 m) tall and 23 to 30 feet (7–9 m) long. That is about as big as a school bus. *Stegosaurus* weighed about 6,800 pounds (3,100 kg). A large rhinoceros weighs about that much.

Stegosaurus was related to earlier dinosaurs that walked on two legs. That may be why its back legs were longer than its front legs.

Even though *Stegosaurus* was large, it had a small, skinny skull. The dinosaur walked around with its head pointed down. Its head was low to the ground because its front legs were shorter than its back legs. *Stegosaurus's* different-sized legs also caused the dinosaur to move slowly. Scientists first thought that *Stegosaurus* walked with its tail low to the ground. Now they think that *Stegosaurus* walked with its back legs straight and its tail higher in the air.

Two Brains?

Paleontologists in the late 1800s believed *Stegosaurus* had a second brain in its tail. Starting in the early 1900s, that was proven to be false. Scientists now know that *Stegosaurus* had one small brain for its large body. Some scientists say the brain was about the size of a walnut or lime. Other experts think it was a little bigger and shaped like a bent hot dog.

Stegosaurus also had small teeth. It was an **herbivore**. It did not need sharp teeth or a powerful jaw to chew up meat. Instead, *Stegosaurus* bit plants and pulled its head back. Its teeth ripped the leaves off. This dinosaur probably did not chew its food. Instead, it used its stomach to break down the food.

The Roofed Lizard

Stegosaurus was known as the "roofed lizard." Scientists once thought that the plates running along its spine and tail laid flat, similar to shingles on a house. But it was later found that *Stegosaurus's* plates stood up straight along its back.

An artist showed what *Stegosaurus* might have looked like if its plates laid flat on its body. This idea has been proven false.

These plates are also called scutes. They had a purpose. Some scientists believe that male *Stegosaurus* used their plates to attract mates.

Scientists still do not agree on the purpose of *Stegosaurus's* plates.

Other scientists think that *Stegosaurus* used the plates to recognize others as the same species.

In 2010, scientists came up with another idea. They thought that the plates were used to control the dinosaur's body temperature. Each plate could help move blood through *Stegosaurus's* large body. This may have helped keep the dinosaur the right temperature.

PRIMARY SOURCE

Matt Carrano is the Smithsonian museum's dinosaur **curator**. He says that the **anatomy** of *Stegosaurus* is still a mystery:

> There's a lot about their anatomy that, while we know what it looks like . . . we don't know how it works.

Source: Maddie Burakoff. "Meet the Dinos of 'Deep Time.'" *Smithsonian Magazine*, 3 June 2019, smithsonianmag.com. Accessed 12 July 2023.

Comparing Texts

Think about the quote. Does it support the information in this chapter? Or does it give a different perspective? Explain how in a few sentences.

The Natural History Museum in London, England, displays the most complete *Stegosaurus* skeleton yet discovered.

CHAPTER 3

FOSSIL FINDINGS

Most *Stegosaurus* fossils have been found in the modern-day United States, including in Utah, Colorado, Wyoming, and South Dakota. There have also been *Stegosaurus* fossils found in China and Portugal.

Some fossilized footprints show researchers that *Stegosaurus* traveled in herds. Several sets of footprints have been found together.

Scientists also learn about *Stegosaurus* through other dinosaurs' fossils. Paleontologists found an *Allosaurus* tailbone with a hole the size of a *Stegosaurus's* tail spike. This fossil shows that *Stegosaurus* defended itself using its spikes.

Bob Simon was president of the Virginia Dinosaur Company. In 2003, he uncovered the most complete *Stegosaurus* skeleton ever found. It was discovered in Wyoming. More than 90 percent of its bones were found. Only the left front leg and the base of the tail were missing. It went on display at the Natural History Museum in London, England, in 2014.

The Morrison Formation is an area of land where many dinosaur fossils have been found. Scientists discovered important *Stegosaurus* fossils there.

Fossils of a young *Stegosaurus* were found in Carnegie Quarry at Dinosaur National Monument in 1977. Paleontologists found limb bones, shoulder blades, skull pieces, hip bones, and ribs. But they did not find any plates. This tells researchers that young *Stegosaurus* may not have had them. Other fossils show that the plates along an adult *Stegosaurus's* back were

Too Many Bones!

Paleontologist Earl Douglass worked in Carnegie Quarry. He was looking for bones of long-necked dinosaurs. But all he could find were *Stegosaurus* bones. He said the *Stegosaurus* bones were in his way. A few nearly complete *Stegosaurus* skeletons were eventually made from the fossils in the quarry.

Stegosaurus does not fight King Kong in the 1933 movie. But images showed the creatures together.

attached to skin, not to bone. Scientists drew this conclusion because fossils of the plates were found separate from the body of the dinosaurs.

Stegosaurus on Screen

Information from fossils has helped people make *Stegosaurus* look accurate in the media. *Stegosaurus* plays a part in the 1933 movie *King Kong*. In this movie, the *Stegosaurus* looks similar to how scientists picture the dinosaur.

People can visit dinosaur parks that show model dinosaurs.

The *Stegosaurus's* spikes stand up tall on its back. It walks with its head close to the ground. But it holds its tail too low. Also, there were eight spikes on its tail in the movie. Now, scientists think there were only four.

Stegosaurus was also in the second and third *Jurassic Park* movies. The dinosaur looks accurate in these movies. *Stegosaurus* are seen in herds. They also defend themselves with their spikes in the films. However, the movie spells their name wrong. A room in the Jurassic Park lab is labeled *Stegasaurus* instead of *Stegosaurus*.

There is a lot of information available about these dinosaurs. But there is still so much more to learn about *Stegosaurus*. Paleontologists will continue to study these creatures in the years to come.

Explore Online

Visit the website below. Does it give any new information about *Stegosaurus* fossils that wasn't in Chapter Three?

A *Stegosaurus* Brought to Life

abdocorelibrary.com/stegosaurus

DINO DETAILS

Spikes on the tip of the tail to fight off predators

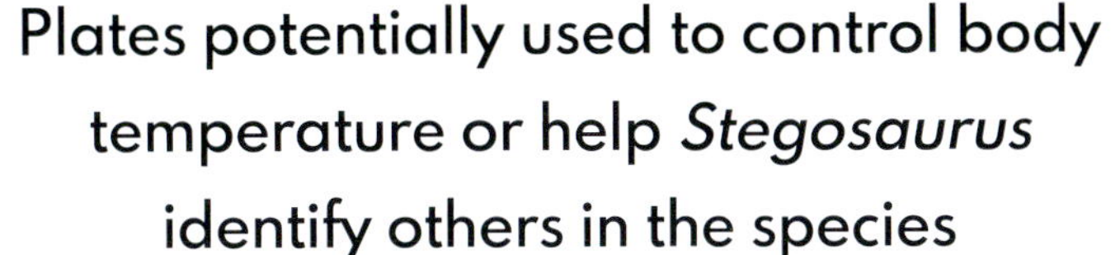
Plates potentially used to control body temperature or help *Stegosaurus* identify others in the species
Small head pointed downward due to its longer back legs
Slow-moving due to its different-sized front and back legs

Glossary

anatomy
the makeup of a body

curator
a person who manages a place with exhibits

extinct
no longer exists

fossil
the remains of a very old animal or plant

herbivore
an animal that eats only plants

herd
a group of animals that travel together

paleontologist
a scientist who studies fossils

predator
an animal that hunts other animals

Online Resources

To learn more about *Stegosaurus*, visit our free resource websites below.

Visit **abdocorelibrary.com** or scan this QR code for free Common Core resources for teachers and students, including vetted activities, multimedia, and booklinks, for deeper subject comprehension.

Visit **abdobooklinks.com** or scan this QR code for free additional online weblinks for further learning. These links are routinely monitored and updated to provide the most current information available.

Learn More

An, Priscilla. *Brachiosaurus*. Abdo, 2024.

Chinsamy-Turan, Anusuya. *Dinosaurs and Other Prehistoric Life*. DK, 2021.

Hulick, Kathryn. *Dinosaurs*. Abdo, 2023.

Index

About the Author

Steph Giedd is a former high school English teacher turned editor. Originally from southern Iowa, Giedd now lives in Minneapolis, Minnesota, with her husband, daughter, and pets.